# WILD CALM

## *A Direct Approach to Happiness*

## by Tim Grimes

For more information visit:

# www.radicalcounselor.com

## Bulk purchases and speaking

For discounts on bulk purchases, or to invite Tim to speak at your next event, email _radicalcounselor@gmail.com_.

ISBN-13: 978-1532703935
ISBN-10: 1532703937

Printed in the United States of America

# A personal message from Tim

Don't believe anything I say just at face value. Test it for yourself. If you test it, you'll see if it really works for you – or not. I feel confident that what I'm about to share with you will work, but don't listen to me. Listen to yourself.

# Contents

# Introduction

This brief, gentle guide isn't your typical advice on how to become happy. That's because the recommendations in here aren't theoretical. Abstract advice on happiness can be a wonderful thing – but this guide is different.

The reason we won't be going over anything abstract involving happiness is because those lofty ideas can confuse us a lot of the time. I know I spent *a long time* confusing myself over the idea of happiness, and I imagine many of you reading this have had similar struggles. Here's the good news: that difficulty and sense of confusion is completely unnecessary.

This guide is intended as an antidote for that confusion. Like I said, for many years, the idea of happiness confused me. Back then, I was willing to go to extreme lengths to hopefully create more happiness in my life. That meant psychedelic drugs and esoteric literature in high school, daily meditation in college, living at a remote Zen Buddhist center after school, and meeting with various self-help teachers throughout my twenties.

This entire journey, though, led nowhere.

In the back of my mind, I think I knew that any "spiritual quest" I undertook to find more happiness would get me nowhere – but nonetheless I plodded along. For years. I'm sure many of you can relate. It's not necessarily the specific people, concepts, or places we seek out that matter, but this *idea* of externally looking for something better. It seems almost normal to be searching for happiness in such a way, because happiness often seems to be so close…yet we can't hold onto it.

Anyway, for me, after about 15 years of searching, I finally stopped. I stopped because I realized I was full of shit. I also realized that I was *already* as happy as I ever needed to be.

Many mundane events led up to this realization, and honestly none of them mean much. The only important takeaway I would like to share with you here – the entire point of this guide – is that if you stop taking your thoughts so seriously, you become a happier person.

Not taking your thoughts seriously isn't an abstract theory. That's why it's worth knowing about, and why we're going to be exploring it. I like being serious. I think it's good to be serious, and it makes you a lovely human being. I also still like reading self-help books and spiritual literature. But, at the same time, you should know that when you feel bad – if you feel bad – you can *immediately* feel better if you just stop taking your thinking seriously. There's nothing particularly special or magical about this...*it just always works.*

Key

This guide is going to show you how to stop taking your [*my*] thoughts as seriously, and immediately become happier by doing that. It involves *physical* action, not just mental action. It's one thing for us to say "stop being serious," and another thing altogether to *do it*. If we're feeling bad, anxious, depressed, or nervous, simply telling ourselves not to be serious won't work. What will work is *physically* addressing our mental state.

Everything we experience emotionally – our entire personal world – comes from our thoughts. Without thoughts, "you" don't exist. If this seems difficult to understand – or idiotic – it'll strike a much deeper chord once you begin doing some of the simple exercises I'm about to describe. These fun exercises are a gateway to a calmer, less stressful life. So test them out!

Again, there's nothing wrong with being serious. There's absolutely nothing wrong with being upset, angry, or sad. This guide isn't telling you to eliminate *any* of those feelings from your life. But what it's going to do is give you a *real* option for how to quickly alleviate those feelings if you don't want them here in this moment.

There's zero pressure on you as you read these suggestions, and you can contact me if you have questions about the material. There also are video tutorials you can watch over at _www.stopbeingserious.com_. I recommend checking out those videos when you have the time.

Without further ado, let's simplify happiness.

## The physical connection between our thoughts and emotions

Happiness, in basic terms, is realizing that you *already* possess all that you could ever need and want. That might sound like New Age mumbo-jumbo. But it's not. It's just the plain truth, when we manage to strip away all the bullshit.

However, I don't care if you believe me yet – because hopefully you'll get to experience this for yourself in the next couple of minutes. But before we get to that, it helps to acknowledge that we're often taught it's not right to feel comfortable in our own skin. There's constantly a subtle nudge to try to "improve" ourselves. Unfortunately, that's usually hard to do – and stressful – as most of us know all too well. So, for at least the moment, I suggest you *stop trying*.

We can't improve our emotions, nor do we need to. Emotions are just *there*. So happiness is nothing we need to seek to improve upon. Paradoxically, if we're able to fully let go of our obsession with "becoming" happy, or improving ourselves, then we actually *will be* happy. That's

*Let Go*

because when we let go of expectations, we naturally embrace what we already are. And we'll come to realize that what we already are is more than enough.

How can we easily embrace what we already are? The answer is deceptively simple:

*By playing around.*

The false need to change things and stressfully improve ourselves comes from our thinking. So, if our thoughts are bothering us, *it's time to dismiss the validity and seriousness of them.*

How we feel and what we think is highly contingent on our body, and certain physical behaviors we've become accustomed to performing. We usually stand the same way, talk the same way, and move around in the same way. Probably the fastest method to change our thinking is just to *playfully disrupt* our normal physical patterns.

*Key*

Here are some examples of playful disruption: moving our body around in a silly way, talking in a funny voice, spinning in circles, jumping up and down, making sounds like a bird, singing in a shrill voice...or anything else that strikes us as childlike or kind of absurd. The options are open-ended and entirely flexible.

By doing something *noticeably different* from our normal physical behavior, we immediately alter our thinking patterns, and become more comfortably aligned with the present moment.

*And this makes us feel very good.*

Everything emotionally – both good and bad – stems from our thinking, and when we momentarily move our bodies around outrageously, we realize this fact for ourselves. *All of a sudden, our thinking changes, and we feel better.* We suddenly feel unburdened. Our stressful thoughts have promptly disappeared.

At first this realization can come as a big surprise. That's to be expected. We've rediscovered something about our mind/body relationship that we've largely been unaware of since childhood: By moving our body around, we can *directly* affect our thinking in a positive way.

Key

*It is, in short, impossible to be seriously worried about anything when we put our wholehearted effort into being physically playful.*

This is the reality of our evolutionary biology and how we think as humans. If you suspect it sounds simplistic, New-Agey, stupid, or too good to be true…you simply haven't tested it for yourself yet.

This works. It *really* works. And it's a hell of a lot of fun.

All of our problems – even bodily issues – originate directly from our thinking. *Our thoughts make us who we are.* By momentarily totally disrupting our accustomed physical behavior, we become aware of this on an innate level, and it shifts everything within us.

The entire process, like I said, is fast and simple. We just need to grant ourselves permission to have fun with our bodies and voices. We have to be serious about not being serious! If we put one hundred percent effort into doing something unusual with our body, our thinking has no other option but to change alongside it.

To be clear – if we start twirling around in circles, or hopping up and down quickly, or doing something similarly strange with our body – we're dramatically deviating from our standard physical movements. If we start talking in a very high voice, or make snorting noises like a pig, we're verbally doing something *totally* different than what we regularly do. If we swing our arms around wildly, or make funny movements with our face, we're doing physical actions we essentially never do.

By explicitly behaving in such an outlandish fashion for a short period of time – whether through our movements, voices, or gestures – we quickly eliminate all the stressful thoughts and feelings that have accumulated in our mind. We're still the same responsible, caring person – it's just that, all of a sudden, we no longer feel stuck with anxious or depressing thoughts. *They've disappeared.*

## Test it for yourself

Becoming friendly with our thinking is much easier if we stop taking it as seriously. We don't need to be moving around or be making funny noises to foster this friendly relationship – but it certainly helps. Moving around, talking in a funny voice, being playful – these are simple, natural things to do when we're enjoying life. There's a reason kids play around so much. It's because it feels good.

Often, our body and mind need to physically 'warm up' before it can stop being so serious. If we jump around for two seconds, and then stop, we haven't put our complete effort into it. We need to let the physical process play out fully by performing these actions for more than just five or ten seconds. If we truly get into our playfulness – whether it's physical or verbal – after only a minute or two we'll find ourselves in a better emotional place.

Don't let limitations with your body get in the way. Whether you're eight or ninety-eight years old, you can do this. *Anybody* can do it. If you're only able to move your hands in a funny way, because of physical constraints, the mental results will still be the same as if you jumped all over the place – as long as you're putting your full effort into it.

*And the results will come quickly.*

If you feel self-conscious behaving in such a silly way, do all this in private. There's no need for anyone else to be around, or for anybody else to have any idea what you're doing. If you still feel self-conscious when you're by yourself, it doesn't matter. Just listen to music you like and dance around for a few minutes in a playful manner – that negative self-awareness will quickly fade away and change into something better.

These exercises make us happy because they make us feel *present*. By being completely engaged in our physical behavior, we have no choice but to become present.

Emotionally, this calms us down, even though we're moving around. We recognize the joy of feeling fully present, *and that joy is fulfilling in itself*. "Now" is happening again and again and again.

We've allowed ourselves to acknowledge the current moment, free of any painful mental projections of the past or future.

There's nothing esoteric about what I'm talking about here. If it sounds esoteric, it means you haven't tested it out yet. This is just your reality when you're enjoying right now.

*Over thinking can be Over Stinking*

*A few questions and answers*

*What does it mean to stop being serious?*

It just means being present by being playfully alive. Basically, we're utilizing a very direct approach in order to feel happier right away. As adults we love to use indirect, philosophical approaches for happiness – this is the exact opposite.

*Act*

You just physically *do it*. And anybody can do it, because it relies on the fundamental truth that we, as human beings, are naturally content when we're not overly bothered by our thinking. We're in pain because we usually become too wrapped up in our thoughts, and take ourselves way too seriously. That's what we have a tendency to do. And not being serious allows you to explore what happens when you're *not* wrapped up.

So the whole idea is very simple. Too simple, actually. Most people don't initially understand this concept. They think it seems too obvious or easy. But that's the whole point. It *is* obvious and easy, and it works.

19

*What are some examples of how to be less serious?*

You can move your body around in a silly way. You might hop up and down like a bunny, or make funny sounds like a baby – anything that disrupts your normal idea of what being a grown-up adult is supposed to be like. Talking in a wacky voice or rolling around on the floor makes you shed that perception pretty quickly. It's liberating.

*Why do you call yourself a "Radical Counselor"?*

I just started calling myself that because it seemed appropriate for the type of advice I was giving. I mean, this was *not* normal advice – it did seem radical and different. So that's where that term comes from, but I don't want it to confuse people. This is important to understand: Anybody can make this stuff work for them by themselves. You definitely don't need to seek out a teacher to learn it. It's natural and intuitive. You don't need to learn anything special from anybody else.

*How is this different than other self-improvement techniques?*

Well, it definitely strikes me as more informal than most advice you hear. I'm a huge fan of practical self-improvement, but often that advice seems to be...so serious. It's usually a bit too stuffy, in my opinion. And because it's like that, it's hard to *actually* apply it to your daily life, at least in my experience. That unnecessary formality stifles its long-term effectiveness.

Not being serious, on the other hand, is wild and loose. You physically *feel* how free it is, and you enjoy yourself because of that. It's more directly intuitive than most kinds of meditation, therapy, self-improvement, or whatever. So you want to keep doing it over a long period of time, because it feels so intuitive and natural.

*When you say more intuitive, what do you mean?*

*It's more fun*. You don't think too much; you just do it. And you have enough faith in yourself that you'll naturally do the right thing. If I see an old lady on the train, I naturally offer her my seat. I don't have to think about it. If I see a child, I smile. It's like that. We already *know* what to do. We don't need to get confused by being too serious about it.

*Do you think it's bad to be serious?*

Not at all. Actually, I think it's probably good to be serious. I'm a very serious person most of the time!

The issue we have is *we don't know how to shut off this seriousness*. Let's be honest – most of us don't have any idea how to really shut it off. I like to say that adults have forgotten how to have fun. We don't remember. That's dangerous for our mental health.

*Do you think some people are afraid that if they do the things you recommend, they'll seem like they've lost their minds?*

Probably. We're all maybe a little afraid of that at first, afraid of acting silly and out of our physical comfort zone. That passes. Acting "crazy" makes you a sane person pretty quickly. It's like if you know how to go up the mountain, you'll know how to get back down.

I should mention, in my opinion, that this seems a lot less crazy than getting up every morning and deciding to go to a job you hate, for instance. Being playful helps restore some *real* sanity back into your life, hopefully. When we physically experiment with our body by moving around differently, we might look slightly crazy, but we're actually very much in control the whole time.

And we can do these things in private. No one has to see us, unless we choose to be seen.

*How would you recommend someone start?*

Just do something wacky, or make an odd facial expression. It's not hard. Start talking in a funny voice, or spinning in circles, or barking like a dog. If you do this with all your effort for just a few minutes, you can't help but feel better. If you have questions, watch the "Stop Being Serious" videos online. I show plenty of different examples of how to start. It doesn't matter what you do, as long as you put effort into it.

*Why do you say it's about embracing who you already are?*

Because that's exactly what we're doing. When we start to behave more playfully, our lives change. We realize that there's really *nothing* wrong with us. We'll stop feeling as judgmental towards others, and we'll be less bothered by events outside of our control.

The real problems start within; they *are not* external. Once we become aware of this, we handle bad situations differently. By being playful, we feel more present. Then we're able to handle adverse situations in a more spontaneous way, and it's usually a lighter and more compassionate way than how we handled them before.

*Why can we handle these bad situations better than before?*

Because we see that our problems really come from our thoughts. Obviously, religions like Christianity and Buddhism have been saying this stuff for eons, but spiritual wisdom often lacks meaning because it seems to be removed from everyday reality.

But you *literally* realize this truth for yourself by not being serious, and being playful. By being playful, you begin to recognize that every one of your problems *originates* from your thinking. So you can solve a problem, at least emotionally, just by handling your thinking differently. This makes you handle negativity and bad situations better than before. And the change in your mindset can lead to other positive results, maybe far exceeding what you'd expect.

*Anything else you'd like to add?*

Have fun! This stuff works. We forget how nice we *inherently* are. It's really just our thinking that scares us so much. So, if you're confused, stop being so serious. Stop trying, and start relaxing instead. Don't think, move! Have some fun. Great things can happen when you allow yourself that option.

### Helpful physical guidelines to be less serious

Here are a few tips on how to be physically and verbally playful. These are just guidelines to help you get started. Once you begin doing this stuff, you'll naturally get the hang of it quickly.

- The main thing is to have fun. Relax and enjoy yourself!

- In terms of moving our body, all we have to do is loosely move around playfully. This can mean jumping up and down, spinning in circles, making strange leg or arm motions, etc. It can be anything that's silly for our body to normally be doing.

- Obviously, most of us wouldn't usually spin around in circles – so that's a good example of moving around. Act a little bit ridiculous, and out of your normal physical comfort zone. Have fun. Be wild. Dance around. If you start moving and you feel awkward, keep on moving.

- After a minute or two of freely moving about, you won't feel awkward. Your body will be working too hard for this awkwardness to remain. Just give one hundred percent effort to the physical action of these funny movements, and your stress will disappear within a few minutes. Often it helps to be playing music you like while doing this.

- If you have serious physical restraints, or the space you're in is so small it makes moving difficult, just move as best you can. The movements can be big or small, as long as the full effort is there.

- We can't think too seriously when we vigorously move. By doing these intensive movement-based exercises, we recognize this. We'll see that our emotional suffering is coming from our overly serious thoughts.

- It can be helpful to make noises, or sounds, when moving around. Just do whatever feels natural, and simultaneously is slightly ridiculous. It's like joyfully dancing. Make as much of a scene as you want.

- You can do all these playful movements alone if you don't want anybody else to see you. It can be completely private, if you wish. No one else has to know about it.

- You can also do this with other people if you want. Whatever works for you, do it. Just give *yourself over to the physical activity, and you'll immediately see the positive mental results!*

- *Moving playfully around can feel amazing, and I generally encourage people to try moving around before they start playing with just their voice. It's very gratifying to suddenly experience your body overtaken with unrestrained, joyful movement.*

- *Making silly faces and noises is easy to do. We don't always have enough room to playfully move all over the place. But we can make funny noises and faces anywhere.*

- *Making funny noises just means talking in a completely absurd way, or making silly sounds. You might bark like a dog, talk like a baby, sound like an old man, or communicate only in grunts. You can contort your face playfully. These noises are about taking your serious thoughts less seriously by making sounds that you'd never normally make.*

- *Playful verbal activities can be done alone, with a partner, or with a group.*

- *Either speaking to yourself, or to a partner or group, start making funny noises. These can be unintelligible noises, like sounds a chicken or* donkey would make, or actual conversations performed in ridiculous sounding tones.

- Don't use any type of voice that you could ever take seriously. You should, ideally, sound ridiculous.

- If we're using a funny voice effectively we can discuss difficult topics and even those subjects won't bring us down. By acting so absurd with our voice and language, we cut through the entire concept of seriousness or "mature" conversation. This is a great way to immediately lighten up.

- You can have a running conversation with yourself in a funny voice, or speak to a friend in an absurd way. Many of you might already do something like this anyway – it's natural. For instance, think about how adults make silly noises when they interact with babies.

- We become aware that absurd voices and noises can actually be a tool to eliminate stress.

- Playful, irreverent self-talk is fun and liberating. You can push your boundaries with it. Don't be afraid to speak gruffly out loud to yourself, and don't be afraid to not make any "sense" while doing it.

- By speaking out loud – instead of keeping your conversations internal – you shift the dynamics of your self-talk. Speaking out loud lets you see your "serious" internal dialogue from a completely different angle, and therefore it diminishes its emotional power over you.

- If you talk in funny voices, you realize you can't mentally suffer over a problem if you're not overly serious about it. Be as serious as you want, but if you feel stressed, try funny voices and/or playfully moving around to get rid of these negative feelings.

- You definitely don't have to perform these exercises to be "in the moment." But, in my experience, these exercises are a very fast and effective way of getting into the moment. If we're present, we're happy. This happiness is profound, because it's a joy that's not seeking anything outside itself, and is fulfilled by being present. It's a mind at ease.

- It's also a mind that has transcended its fearful thinking, and recognizes that individual thoughts aren't the problem, but that taking them seriously can certainly make them appear to be a problem.

- We're invigorated when we're not overwhelmed with our thoughts; we're easily uplifted and energetic. Children are a great example of this. They're bundles of energy and love just playfully moving around. They're active, naturally curious, and eager to explore their surroundings. Kids often may have no set idea of what they're doing, but they do it joyfully.

- Children have so much energy and enthusiasm because they're more physically present than we usually are as adults. Kids aren't as easily overcome by their thinking; they intuitively know that by moving around and playing, they'll feel better. It's gradually, through social indoctrination, that they become increasingly self-aware of "who" they are, and stop being as playful.

- The problems most of us face come from a lack of playfulness, because the playfulness I'm referring to isn't a light or trivial thing. We need to feel fulfilled, and have a sense of peace in the present moment, in order to be happy. Playfulness allows us to reconnect with that present moment.

Wunderbar

toot toot

Tootsie GOODBYE

Mammy

BO Jangals
Dancer

# *Wild Calm*

## Keynote or Workshop

## Stop Being Serious with Tim Grimes

**Tim Grimes** *speaks authoritatively on topics centered around stress relief, work-life balance and personal fulfillment. Based upon his unique background and experience, Tim shares surprising ways for everyone to become more productive and fulfilled by embracing relaxation as a paradigm for success.*

To invite Tim to speak at your next event, email:

*radicalcounselor@gmail.com*

**Other guides from Tim:**

RELAX MORE, TRY LESS
*The Easy Path to Abundance*

MINDFUL MANIFESTATION
*A Uniquely Effective Way to Practice Mindfulness*

MANIFESTATION THROUGH RELAXATION
*A Guide to Getting More by Giving In*

For more information visit:

**www.radicalcounselor.com**

Made in the USA
Middletown, DE
24 June 2020